10

Table of Contents

Introduction

For leaders or those who aspire to be leaders, what I have to say is not necessarily meant to convince you of anything. However, it is intended to take you on a journey that hopefully inspires you to reinvigorate your approach to anything you desire to achieve out of life. We lead in all parts of life, whether indirectly or directly. The way we seek to be intentional about taking ownership of the state of our livelihood as a whole can make all the difference in what often feels like a long haul.

Nevertheless, the haul is worth every effort if we have fundamental commitments toward succeeding at our ambitions pursuits towards a purpose. This book is not intended to be an essay or dissertation packed with a variety of research re-written to give it a fresh perspective. Not to be mistaken, the studies and principal evaluations and analysis of best leadership practices are necessary and essential. Every leader needs a pathway, and enrichment through the work of others is invaluable.

Nonetheless, the message in this book serves to speak to the heart and mindset; to challenge the pathway of leadership that exist without the audacity to feel for others in a way that may be contrary to self. This selfless state is a requirement of leadership; especially, in education. There is not a single person in the profession of education who is not called upon to be a servant leader to others in some capacity. For leaders, this calling and the expectations that come with it is in multiplicity every day. Leaders can decide to follow a pathway that does not encompass heart and mindset; but, if they do, they are bound to leave their best self behind.

I have come to believe that the only way to fail at anything is to acknowledge that failure is one of two outcomes in everything we do in life. I can recall the first day I entered the classroom as a middle school teacher. I was so full of novice expectations, and clueless to the what and how of being a teacher. However, the one thing that I had under my belt was that I believed I could make a difference. I didn't exactly know what that difference would be, or how I would get to it. I just knew the belief was internal.

There is nothing profound about a person entering a career and believing that the work they are about to embark upon could be life-changing. However, the ardent artifacts of our life become a reality when the belief begins to take fruition. The state of any prelude in our lives starts with an idea, and if we are wise enough and enjoy a bit of luck- the end of our journey (that feeling we internalized at our prelude) will be evergreen throughout our lives.

10 is partly a memoir of my professional journey and a manifestation of my belief that my 'why' has always been to allow my heart and mind to coexist in my pathway towards accomplishments. If nothing else, I hope anyone who desires to lead and be an inspiration to anyone or cause in their life, find reflection in the ten chapters dedicated to this book.

Your 'why' belongs to you; and, your pathway to your 'why' is unique to your journey. You have to know how you got there, and hopefully make it worthwhile for yourself and others.

Part 1: My Journey Forward

Chapter 1: The Beginning

In May of 2006, a week before my college graduation, I interviewed for my first teaching job at a middle school. I was clueless about how to prepare for this interview. My pathway before the moment I realized I wanted to teach, was to exit my undergraduate and become a writer. One day, about a month before I graduated it dawned on me that my pathway to becoming a writer was morbid. In retrospect, I had done nothing besides attend classes and set myself up to earn enough credits to graduate with a degree in Literary Studies; sprinkled with some intense creative writing classes.

Thus, as this prelude of entering college was coming to an end, I had important decisions to make. At the time, I was a team lead at a large sunglass corporation. I enjoyed working with other people, and there was something about satisfying a customer that bought me instant gratification. I was sure of two things at age 22: 1.) I loved writing, and 2.) I enjoyed working with and leading other people.

I was a bystander in a random conversation about the future goals of students that I'd never met at my university when I heard someone mention going into an alternative certification program to become a teacher. I had no idea what that meant, but I was instantly intrigued by the notion. Why had I not thought of this before? Teaching was like leading, and how awesome would it be to teach students how to write? As a bonus, I would get the opportunity to work with other teachers. In my mind, it was a win-win and the best decision I could make at that point in my life.

So, within days I took a leap of faith. I signed up for an Alternative Certification program and submitted a series of inexperience applications for teaching positions. I mentioned luck in the introduction because I had not walked across the graduation stage, taken any certification test, nor entered into the first day of my Alternative Certification program when I got my first call for an interview.

My interview was at a middle school in a growing district outside of the Houston area. I put together what was likely the cheesiest portfolio I could conduct by the results of my Google search of "what to bring to an interview for being a teacher." My interview was with the principal of the campus. No committee. No extra leg work to get the job. I cannot remember much about the interview, other than I recall the principal complimenting me on my attire. She never looked at the portfolio I brought, and the only question to my recollection that was "meaty" was, "Do you like kids"? Point blank. I said, "Absolutely!"

Moreover, I proceeded to go on this passionate rant that I walked away regretting because she ended the interview after that; thus, I figured I blew it. Twenty-eight hours later, five days before my undergraduate graduation, and two weeks before the start of my certification program- I was offered a middle school teacher/coach position — insane luck and timing.

My first year of teaching wasn't typical. It was incredible. Finding your fit is paramount. Not just in your career path, but your life path. The most successful people in life and relationships are those who saw their fit: the best match for their self. Every job, affiliation, or position we go for or even successfully achieve in the beginning may not be our best fit. Where I landed my first year as a teacher was an excellent fit for me, and because of this, I thrived early. By the end of my first year, the opportunity to take on the girl's coordinator position at the middle school before ultimately taking an assistant coach position at the high school. I leaped forward at a baffling speed considering all the factors that should have made it much more difficult for me to spring forward in the manner that I did. The question I always asked myself was, "Did I earn it?".

When I separated this notion of guilt that the only way to earn opportunity was to put in x amount of years, I realized that the superiors in my life at the time recognized my potential and my talent. They took a leap of faith on me, despite the rigid perceptions of how and why any should earn opportunities to move forward. I've carried their wisdom with me all these years.

My accomplishments have always been a ricochet effect: Surround myself with the right people, be good at not only what I do but how I do it, and be willing to accept success more than failure- flourish. The most straightforward cycle of ingredients in my beliefs paid off. To top it off, my passion for teaching kids grew.

By year five, I still felt fresh and alive. I wanted more and more out of my career, and achieving was non-negotiable. When I became a head coach, I begin to look at leadership in a vastly different light. Some people attempt to lead with their title and others lead with their heart and mind; the title is just the aspect that gives you certification to take on the responsibility of the role. The more I committed to the ownership of my program, the more I realized the only way to build a dynamic program was to grow the people around me. Whether we won or lost every game, the program wouldn't be worthy of anything without great teachers and leaders serving kids to the best of our ability.

By year two, I had a different approach to my leadership. I wanted the same expectations that I carried for my accomplishments to serve others in finding theirs. I became more intentional about helping my coaches find their passion and purpose for growing. To grow, you have to have a desire to do so; but, to develop others you have to seek to understand who they are and what they aspire to be.

This newfound passion of my own inspired me to go back to school for my Masters in Administration and Leadership. I wasn't quite ready to throw in the towel on coaching and teaching, but I knew I wanted to continue to educate myself on leadership and position myself to have the opportunity to go into another facet of education at some point in my life.

One definition of a prelude is the beginning of a piece of music, and the moment that I realized this beautiful and rewarding song that I had the privilege to live within for years of my career was coming to a postlude, I knew it was time for me to take a leap of faith of my own. If moments are meant to give you pause and clarity, I have had my fair share.

It was during the very last playoff game of my basketball coaching career. I happened to be coaching against a group of girls that I'd coached at a former campus. It was a remarkably challenging moment; on one end I am rooting for my current team to win the game while beginning in awe of the team that I had the privilege to coach in the past. There were moments during that game that felt like slow motion. It was the point that I knew my team was going to lose and I looked into the crowd and saw my nephew, a few months old at the time, I saw the end of a part of my career that brought me great purpose. It was bittersweet, and still is to this day because anything that impacts your life the way that my years of teaching and coaching did never indeed leaves you. Always, I carry everything I learned from the coaches, teachers, students, parents, and leaders from that part of my career with me.

Like most things in life, there was no guarantee that I would get an Assistant Principal position. After all, I was terrible at politicking and networking. As such, I'd done a poor job of sustaining relationships with the people I'd work for or within the past.

My reputation and my resume were the most substantial elements I had when I applied for the Assistant Principal position, ironically at the high school in which I'd been a previous head coach. Once again, I had some excellent favor stacked in my deck. The principal that hired me in the head coach position was now the Human Resource Director in the district. Not to mention, she was someone that challenged me to go back to school and get my Masters. So, I got a chance to interview for the position. The blessing of circumstances is real.

At the time, I didn't know that I would be sitting on a two-panel interview of the new high school in the district, as well. The new high school was the feeder campus to the middle school that I had my very first job in the district. I was fortunate to have some real experience and understanding of the vastly different sides of the district and could speak to that well.

A few days after the interview, I got a call from my former principal, now Human Resource director, that in a

11

few days they would officially offer my name to the board for the assistant principal position at the new high school.

Recall, I abandoned the" did I earn it" question long before this moment. However, I had to acknowledge that I did earn it through the work, commitment, and sacrifices I made to get to that moment. Moreover, I had to recognize that to keep what I'd earned I had to see it as another prelude that was worth every bit of passion and purpose that I came into education bestowing. I earned it, and I wanted it to matter.

To understand and value your why, you have to reflect on how you got to where you are. Our pathway forward should have meaning, and if it doesn't, we have to ask ourselves why. The likelihood that you may have left something of yourself behind if you can't recollect the purpose of why you've done anything is high. If we leave anything of ourselves behind, it should never be the passion that drove us to purpose in the first place. We should never surrender the best parts of ourselves for the gratification of attaining a title.

The title will come, almost naturally, through our dedication to be the best we can be for ourselves and others. The luck comes from the belief that you can have it because you deserve it. If you solely have to rely on faking it to get to the "top," at some point the person that you frankly are will surface. In leadership, if you can't commit to building the best version of yourself- you certainly will struggle with doing this for others.

Understand your beginning and carry the things that propelled you forward with care.

Chapter 2: More than A Title

The first "crucial conversation" I can recall as an assistant principal was with my principal. She didn't often venture down to my office. The first one-on-one visit we had was about two months after the start of the school year. It wasn't a scheduled visit, so I didn't have time to assess or prepare for the conversation. Most of our conversation was casual; simply a check-in to see how I felt I was doing and if I needed anything. Our discussion trailed off into an awkward silence at one point, and she presented a very pivotal question to me: What do you think the teachers feel about your leadership?

It was a meaningful question that I had not taken the time to reflect on. I think I was more discipline and duty at that point of my role. My response was, "I think they like me." Thinking back that is the most amateur response that I could have given because the fact is I had no clue. When she left, I immediately scheduled a time to visit with my department head one-on-one. I took the same approach my principal did of asking the surface level questions first and offering my support for anything needed.

After our conversation, I felt like the only thing I'd accomplished was a superficial discussion to validate my title. That wasn't good enough, at least for me. From that point on, I set out to be more intentional about getting to know who my teachers were, and most of all how they were serving our students. I did a good enough job for a first-year assistant principal at repositioning myself from being just a title and more of a servant leader, and I likely could have coasted at this level of above average from that point and most of my career as an Assistant Principal. Nevertheless, the gut check that any leader worth their salt should ask themselves is, "If I feel I earned this title, what I have done with it?"

Is our calling to be mediocre, average, or remarkable in life? If we believe it is to be astonishing, we have to be incredibly memorable through the impact that we make in the lives of ours. Having the same breakfast every day of your life can be enjoyable, but not remarkable. Remarkable requires you to step outside the box and challenges yourself at levels that may be incredibly uncomfortable. Being extraordinary at anything demands you to take a risk at times; to fail; to not be loved by everyone- which is an impossible feat.

I made a point to call myself out in the places I was not remarkable. At the same time, my focus became so intense in one area of my life that other areas lost relevance. It took quite some time for me to accept that the areas that lost importance were things that I needed to leave behind because they were holding me back from the leader, the person, and the life that I sought to live.

Again, the research can give you the pathway, but the heart and mind can give you the passion and purpose you need to be remarkable in work that you do. The knowledge can exist without the heart and soul, but the passion and purpose cannot.

The earlier a leader moves past their title, in which they may have the knowledge to perform, the more expeditiously he or she equips themselves with the unteachable tools of inspiring and motivating others. The argument is not that you can't become a leader without the latter; many have achieved it and left any responsibility to call out their heart and mind for what they do behind. The argument is centered around a broader question, "If you achieve a leadership title, is it solely for you or you and others?"

To be a servant leader is to sacrifice yourself, even when yourself needs attention. It's a challenging, yet essential aspect of being a leader. Furthermore, servant leadership requires you to feel beyond the surface level. It requires you to separate yourself from title to collaborator, mentor, coach, and to have sympathy and empathy even when you would instead use the authority of your claim to squash any situation that you defy. There is little point in expending your title in the humiliation of others.

In education, the teacher that receives a bad evaluation, the student that has earned a consequence for their behaviors, or the moment a mistake or choice leads to the end of anything for anyone is not the moment to drive with your entitlement. If anything, the worst of times can often be the most teachable and reflective moments for a leader.

Handling a situation with integrity and grace is far more extensive than the ruthless perception that a leader can leave eyes wide open for others to dissect and make judgments. If anything, the conclusion that you hope those whom you've earned the respect of can draw from any situation that you are involved in, even without knowing all the facts, is that

15

whatever the conclusion they know that you are an upstanding individual and would not seek an adverse outcome unless the outcome was out of your control. Education is a business in which people are the product; albeit, students, parents, staff, and community- who you are as a leader is always on display for scrutiny and admiration. People will care about your title at first, but they will dismiss it when it conflicts with what they need or desire.

The most significant disappointment in my career was the moment I received a 'no' that mattered to me. My second year as an assistant principal, I thought I'd earned enough clout to go for the Associate Principal position on my campus. My non-negotiable attitude for achievement and my reputation for being knowledgeable and supportive of teachers and students, lead me to believe that I had somehow earned the right to leap into the next phase of leadership.

I had encouragement from teachers, my counterparts, parents, and even cabinet members. For the first time in my life, I failed to achieve something that mattered to me. Sure, I got an interview. I even got a face-to-face after-the-fact with the Assistant Superintendent, in which he told me I was a "Rock Star," but this wasn't the position for me.

I vividly recall walking from that meeting and immediately applying for positions that evening, not even in Houston. I was angry; not reflective and unwilling in many ways to accept the idea of failure that I'd never experienced. To be clear, I'd received a few "no callbacks" on my pursuit for positions in education, but never from places or positions that truly mattered to me. The places that I applied to more so to justify that I was making moves or could make moves, I referred to as "fillers"; an attempt to find gratification in my abilities. As luck may have it, the committee did me a favor in not selecting me for the associate position, because their decision was pivotal in steering me to an interview in a prestigious district in Austin, TX.

When I told my principal, I'd applied for a position in Austin and received a call for an interview she was shocked. It dawned on me that I didn't handle my perception of anger and failure as a true professional in this circumstance, as I'd given her no notice that I was seeking another position. In my apologetic release of emotions, she stopped me and said, "I don't care that you applied somewhere else. I am more concerned that you are closing other opportunities that may be a better fit for you in this district."

To me, the opportunity that I thought was the best fit for me had passed, and nothing she said after that moment mattered to me, unfortunately. There I was, a young and ambitious risk taker, being all of the things that had propelled me forward and a crybaby of sorts at the same time. It was the moment that I received an offer for a job at the campus in an Austin district that educators aspire to be a part of, that I understood what failing forward truly meant.

My title wasn't what landed me the job; it only got me to the interview. Timing and luck are what made the opportunity right for me. Most of all, my belief that I deserved something and was passed over for it made me take a risk. What I will never speak of is why my anger and disappointment in not getting the Associate Principal position at the campus in Houston under a microscope of the facts may have real merit, because it sincerely doesn't matter. That wasn't the right fit for me.

I had a choice to accept it and remain an assistant principal at the same campus, pending other opportunities or to leap in forward in a different way; without the network of people and the relationships of reputation to ricochet me forward. I relied on my title to affirm my resume, but I relied on myself to solidify my opportunity. I went into my interview in this prestigious district with my heart on my shoulders and my mind fully open. I wanted to grow and to do so, I had to abandon a community that I'd served seven years of my career in; a place that I called "home" for most of my professional life. I came to my knees when I got the call that moved me to Austin, TX. Though, I carried with me all the sacred lessons, memories, and opportunities that the district and people I served for those years had given me. To this day, it remains my first professional home.

Many carry the title. The title is a credential; the purpose and passion remain the distinction.

Chapter 3: A New Beginning

Movement is highly underrated. Let me caveat this part of the book by giving high praise to those that have been able to stay where they started and grow and advance the way they wanted, and at the pace, they sought. If you've been able to achieve all of the above- you are without a doubt a trailblazer in a rarity of advancement. Thus, my argument or position is not against experience, loyalty, or commitment. However, it is against the notion that if your resume illustrates 'movement,' then you somehow have failed. It's not where you've been that tells the story; it's what you've done where you've been and why you felt the need to move. I've certainly moved throughout my career, but for justifiable reasons.

Had I not, I am not sure I wouldn't have become pigeon-holed in the places that I'd already flourished. The road less traveled is still a road. The key is knowing when you need to step out of your current reality and veer off the beaten path that may very well not be leading you towards your goals. It's a difficult decision; especially in a profession so dominated by relationships and dedication to people. We carry forward, and we leave behind. The fact of educators. Good leaders leave the best of themselves behind for the next, while never losing what made them suitable for what they are leaving behind.

The new me was still the old me, but I had to be better than before. I was tackling a new city, a new district, and a new life. Each blazed alongside the other offering chaos and delight all at once. Our professional experience and our personal life marry in more ways than some care to acknowledge; albeit, the privacy in which we separate the individual from the occupation is paramount. My new beginning was essential to any future goals, and I was entering unknown territory in the literal sense for the first time in my life.

Priority: Learning how to fit in without fitting out, while still holding to who I am. Perhaps, this should have been the definition of insanity for me because to embrace what you don't know or maybe not even agree with requires inordinate sacrifice. Sacrifice is one of the most critical elements of leadership. It is genuinely not teachable it just is. It would be best if you dealt with the "is" to soar past every ounce of your being that wants to fight and defy it.

My new place, encompassing all the above, was a challenge to start. I was dealing with a whole new world; different expectations, different needs, diverse stakeholders, and a completely different viewpoint of who I was. None of the people that I lead or worked with knew me. I entered into a territory, a protectorate of culture and values, that I was more clueless about than I could fathom. The struggle within was excruciating for quite some time. Until, the day that I decided to call out the perceptions and assumptions about me.

I made whom my new environment thought I was fair game. I critiqued myself in a way that I hadn't allowed myself to do in the past, and I welcomed that I had a lot more to learn. Most people only care about where you come from and who you are enough to form an opinion, and from there you have to make who you are and what you are about significant to them; at least that is cognizance of people that a leader should understand.

Leaders can be the givers of critics or critiques, or they can be the facilitators of reflections and determined purpose. How you view, one or the other makes all the difference in how you self-reflect on the necessary assessment of yourself that can bring growth or contentment to your life. I took it on the chin. From the teachers that I supervised, and I made it matter. It wasn't that all they perceived or assumed about who I was as a leader and a person was right- it was that I needed to accept that they had an opinion.

It was an interrogation of myself to see past their judgment that I found unfair or hypocritical and solely focus on what they were communicating about what they needed from me. If what they were lacking made sense in providing for and producing exceptional outcomes for students, I was completely onboard. If it didn't, I stood my ground. I found that when you hold your ground because you have listened first and sought to understand second, people can respect disagreement.

Every resolution doesn't require an agreement; it requires a mutual consensus that all sides had an opportunity to at the least speak their piece and at best have what they felt acknowledged. Acknowledgment is not agreement, but it is a consideration. Opening up to the review of other's thoughts and feelings can be a compelling way for a leader to gain real credibility of their character and judgment. Your backbone as a leader is not an accomplishment achieved through title; the grit of a leaders spine is an illustration shown through experiences and decision making.

I came into my new situation, circumstance, and beginning with some great attributes that I'd carried forward. I also arrived with some qualities of my perceptions and assumptions that I had to leave behind. For me to clutch the possibilities of my new beginning, I had to get over myself. I learned a lot at unhesitating speed; I sought feedback, growth, and wins through pre-determined purpose. I became truly passionate about other people, and not just me. Before, my cup was half full. I wanted teachers to thrive, because when they thrive kids thrive and the organization is cultivated in invigorating passion and purpose.

Not everyone saw my renewed purpose and passion that way. To some, my leadership style still didn't fit what they found important. However, I stood for something, and I knew that what I stood for came with knowledge, heart, and a growth mindset. I was less worried about being loved or admired, and more concerned with being respected and remarkable. I was privileged to carry the great things that people had left behind for me, and I needed to give something back for others to take forward with them. My new beginning taught me that accepting relevant humility can be empowering, as so long as you recognize that it is one of the factors of development that you should never want to ricochet.

Approach your opportunities with an open heart and mind, because it is almost impossible that you won't need to accept some degree of change to be the very best version of yourself for the people who need you to transform the things that they may not apprehend are holding them back.

Chapter 4: Occupational Absorption

There was a point in not just my career, but my life, that I absorbed the areas that I was performing at the average level of my expectations. My bar was not as high as I thought or portrayed it to be For almost a decade of my career. I existed in a half cup filled life, and it took some additional growing pains and leaps of faith to hold me accountable to the expectations of myself. The stage of "occupational absorption" became a matter-of-fact principle for me. I desired to be held responsible for all the confidence and presuppositions that carried me for so long.

A vulnerability is the greatest fixation of growth, and yet the most fearsome of failure. I'd survived year one of the new beginning. There was nothing particularly special about what I'd accomplished that first year; except, that I happened to work for a leader that helped to position me in the face of opportunities. If anyone ever tells you that they made it anywhere without the guidance or influence of someone else, they are either delusional or unsuccessful. The little things mattered in year one of my new beginning. Although, I didn't know it at the time the exposure that I had to present myself, albeit, in attitude, mentality, or ability slowly chipped away at the makings of my future.

I couldn't see any of the experiences that my leader at the time put before me as essential to any progression of my career, because I was still too hung up on what I hadn't achieved and what I didn't have versus what existed before me. Had it not been for my genuine passion for being an educator I would've likely have failed at every aspect of the little things that were conforming bigger things for my future. Occupational absorption was a sort of hazard and intercession of my contemplation of ordinary existence in my professional ambitions. I was at a stop-gap between where I was and where I wished I were, and the only methodology I could see to pull me from this was to take a leap of faith.

This leap required me to attempt once again to leave behind the networking of people, experiences, and possibilities that I'd spent a year (a new beginning year) establishing. I sought movement, and I was unrelenting in finding the opening- not the fit- that would lead me beyond my current role. As luck may have it, I'd made just enough of an impression in what I perceived to be little moments of impact to earn credibility from afar.

The day I received a tap on the shoulder from another leader, whom I never really had the privilege to work directly with, to explore a new potential role catapulted my growth in ways that I am still sprouting from to this day. Timing, people, faith, and drive- occupational absorption; the best hazard I could've had at that point of my life.

For transparency, this new opportunity was not a gift. I had to win over a committee of people who knew nothing about me, other than the words on my resume, and people whom I was unfamiliar. It was the perfect storm of life changes and experiences that helped prepare me for that moment. I got it. I earned it. However, I can't say I was exactly ready for all that it entailed; until I was. On the job training is the only practice that can honestly give you direct responsibility to the duties and capacity of any role that you play. You could be an accomplished person on an individual level and struggle with being a partner to someone else. The learning curve in any role we play in life is a direct attribution to our ability to withdraw from self-comfort enough to embrace the necessity of the assimilation process of taking on the new role; while keeping in mind that what we are assimilating into will require maturation and development to be its most dynamic self.

As we progress in our career, the depreciation of cognitive dissonance between our resistance of occupational evolutions via our stubbornness to change- can bridge together the personal and organizational efficacy that creates true transformation. I never had the chance to see the fullness of this newfound evolutional mindset manifest in the year and a half in my new position as an Associate Principal. Had it not been for that leap of faith and my infatuation at that time in my life with allowing myself to be absorbed in my work in a way that I hadn't been in the past- I likely would not have come to change in mindset that I needed to be a better leader.

Within three years of moving to Austin, I'd advance in my career and received some "No's" along the way. Unlike in years past, the chances I took on the opportunities that I didn't get only made me reflect and grow differently. I wasn't angry or throwing myself a pity party on the few times that I wasn't a "fit," or perhaps ready, for the needs of an organization. The "salt" of great leaders is the appreciation that perfection is not a given nor ever a reality.

There is no perfect self, nor perfect place; however, there are definite opportunities and optimal possibilities to have extraordinary impact. Thus, growth and development is a thickening of conversions of lasting success; great leaders persist at this.

The day that I was named principal of campus was the day that all the things that I'd carried forward from extraordinary people and experiences, the sacrifices and tribulations of my journey, made the most profound impact on my professional life. Getting to that moment was never perfect; and although I'd envisioned it many times before, it was never a reality I could fully grasp- until I did.

Did I earn it? Yes, and, I still am.

Chapter 5: Intuition of the Future

A s I close as much of a concise wrap-up of my journey forward, it comes with the omission of one truism: Nothing I've revealed matters or is worthy of thought, unless you have your reflection and beliefs about your journey. Now, would be a great time to consult yourself on what it is that you want to achieve as you move forward on whatever mission you desire to obtain. What does a vision matter without tracing the footsteps of how you got there and what your pathway ahead could be?

In summary of part 1, I find myself on this amazingly indescribably journey of leading. I have never believed that leadership is about the authority of superiority or being number one, but without a doubt, the duty and responsibility is the "buck stop" of leadership. Nonetheless, there is far more to it than that. The title asserts that you are, the actions assert that you can and will. If you fail at the can and will, you ultimately fail at the title. As Latin philosophical thinker Rene Descartes states, "I think; therefore I am." If you can muster up enough strength and vulnerability to accept that everything that you desire to be is within you, then the fruits of your labor will lead to greater accomplishments and more significant influence.

My past, in more ways than one, has shaped my future. The intuition I have about my journey is that I am on one, and I have been from the beginning of each prelude of my life. I am not as interested in loathing over my failures, because they have happened and will. I am far more interested in relishing in the fact that I can fail and fall forward because I believe that an essential component of progress is addressing our inadequacies. Success is not inevitable; it is prescriptive.

I decided that the doctrine of my occupation is to live within it; whatever role I play. Beyond me, I have to feel what others feel about what they do and why they do it, and I have to have the mindset to want to influence and impact in the same manners or more in which I have been. What is a leader when the mind and the heart do not intertwine in a way that compels others to grow, to change, and to crave passion and purpose for what they do as if their life depended on it? Extreme, perhaps to some. Simpleminded, not.

The intuition that I have about my future is that I have to continue to be intentional and relentless about remarkable impact. I want more than ever to be better at what I do. I wish more than ever to make my "why" resonate through my leadership and influence. I want more than ever to make a difference. The mockery of achievement is defying every single nagging naysayer and antagonist of difference that I have and will continue to face. I chose to acculturate negativity as an infertile part of my growth. I earned this. What I can't accept is that earning it gives me the right to coast back into the mediocracy of myself.

In the next few chapters, I offer those of you still reading the best advice I can give you about the many things I've sprinkled through the first five chapters that have helped me to achieve my goals and continue to propel me forward. Remember to pause to reflect on what I say. Please consult your journey and figure out what matters or is significant to it. Assimilate what matters to you, but while doing so explore the hidden and eyes-wide-open oppositions to your success.

Part II: Earn It

Chapter 6: Stand for Something

E ven the most ruthless dictators stood for something. They had a belief, and they made their belief transparent and tangible to others. Many people fail at achieving their goals because they struggle to apprehend the necessities to be successful within the roles, conformities, and performance required for their aspirations. While some, reach their goals only to find they fall short of the imitation of a persona that they are unable to live up to when the reality of the work at hand absorbs the glamour of the achievement. If you believe in who you are and what you stand for, be immensely careful not to replace you with a version of yourself that never existed. You can find your philosophy on pretty much anything in life in a book or through a Google search, but if you want it to be metamorphic in your growth- you have to make it your own.

There are several ways to discover what your true philosophical beliefs about anything are.

1.)Start with what you don't agree with and scrutinize it.

Agree to disagree with the things that you already think you don't find value or worthiness of thought. Dig deep and consult whether or not these beliefs are worth throwing away because every piece of understanding or knowledge we decide to throw from the purview of our views should bring more value and broader insight to our beliefs and mindset. Acknowledge what you do not think you agree with about your forward progress, and be careful of what you throw away without taking the time to organize the substance, biases, and truths of anything you believe to be fallible.

2.)Know what you are confident in, and accept it into your life credo.

Anyone can say they are about something, but to be confident about it requires a degree of confidence or even cockiness at times to live it out. Consider that no one wants an active shooter around without a confident leader to handle the situation the best that they can. If that statement seemed too extreme or unfathomable to you-you should go back and consult the credibility of your confidence. Of course, the event of an active shooter is an anomaly in even the places that they have taken place, but you have to "go there" in your mindset to lead anyone with astuteness. Stretch the norm and understand the anomalies, so that you can build your awareness of confidence to handle any situation. Confidence exudes a presence that people not only respond to but want to follow. Some may find you intimidating, but even those can accept that you are someone who believes in your capabilities and skillset.

3.)Be aware that you are likely not the only one that believes what you believe.

Thinking back, most of the opportunities I went for and did not achieve likely came from my immaturity in believing that even showing up for the occasion made me somehow special. You have to prepare to be unique before the moment that you have an opportunity to be. There will always be someone else who has a similar belief as you and maybe even lived that belief more than you have. Adversaries of similar goals and aspirations will persistently stand between you and your achievements in some way. Focusing on everyone else doesn't matter in the grand scheme of what will help you capture the moment. However, being able to speak to what makes you unique and knowing that every single opportunity is a building block to a better you, whether you achieve the role that you are going for or not, can bring others into your journey to be trailblazers with you in finding your fit. Leave an impression on the roads you less travel, because those roads are often rare finds of your journey. The prints you leave behind may ricochet you back to the very thing that you were meant to grow.

4.)Own who you are; without regret.

Too many people try to fit into the person they are not, which often places them within circumstances that ultimately drown out the person that they are. Yes, understanding your fit and how to fit into your environment is essential, but not at the extent that you are allowing anyone or anything to devour the best version of you. The only satisfaction that derives from fitting-in is if the fit is right for you; but even then, you will need to be an all-purpose you that can stand out and still feel accepting within your fit. You will never have an all-in of stakeholders, albeit coworkers, family, or friends of who you are. The transverse fact is that you too will not have an all-in belief of others. So, what should anyone expect that of themselves or others? There should be no regret in owning who you are unless you haven't achieved the pathway to be the very best version of yourself. The best of you is a continuance of the evergreen qualities that stick with you from year to year; from inception to inception.

Be deliberate about finding what you stand for. It's not a principle of yourself that can be left behind.

Chapter 7: The Pitfalls of Relationships

T

his chapter may be one of the most critical aspects of all facets of our livelihood and is indeed a topic that has become the universal buzzword of defining the core connections of people to people in arguably every industry that exists. The word 'relationships' is thrown around in the professional setting, especially within education, like the expectations of mash potatoes on an American buffet- you assume they will be there.

I will throw my red flag up to this chapter by confessing that I am likely one of the worse people at sustaining the type of relationships in which one believes that breaking bread, confessing your deepest secrets, and going to happy hours is what defines a meaningful relationship. I like to call the partaking in the aforementioned 'friendships.'

The danger of what relationships are so loosely floating in definition nowadays is that in many circles they are producing irresponsible decision making and require no significant prerequisites to achievement. The viewpoint as mentioned above of relationships is a dangerous pathway for a leader in acquiring achievement. The standard of deviation of relationships in a mass organization is in general: you're either in or out. Leaders who boast their relationships as the vanguards of their success may want to assess their merit.

It is almost offensive for me to make the argument or assertion I just made. I offer this concise explanation: I have relationships with people that have propelled my career forward; I've mentioned this time and time again throughout the book without devoting the focus to relationships. The difference is, I do not see these individuals as my friends or companions; they are highly regarded and respected by me professionally. I do not interact with any of them as I do my friends; I do not seek a leg-up because I know them. I value that they respect who I am and genuinely recognize potential and talent in me. I would take that any day in my professional livelihood over the friend that can't tell me "no" because their judgment is too clouded by our "relationship." Relationships should not be your pitfall of achieving your remarkable you. They should be the most potent identifiable propellers of your growth, without bias or corruption.

I offer these considerations of the relationships you carry forward in your professional livelihood:

1.)Value

The bonds, or networking, that you establish in your professional journey should bring value to your progress. It doesn't mean that you won't run across some professional relationships that ultimately become friendships, but knowing with the tide has changed is important. Friends can bring value to your life, but there is a distinct difference in boarding yourself among relationships versus friendships as you seek to surge to your goals. Friendships can puncture the heart; relationships certainly have an impact, but they are far less costly when the heart is not so entangled that our better judgment becomes hindsight. Leading with your heart and mind also requires guarding the two against the debris of expectation or agendas of others that can potentially harm you.

2.)Separation is Power

When it comes to relationships, the best leaders can separate their admiration for someone, when the moment calls for it. This ability is gravely vital because I would bet in every professional and personal journey there has been moments that someone you cared deeply for has disappointed you. When you are a leader, you have to be the catalyst to situations sometimes that requires you to put your personal feeling aside. The call to action of every leader is a balancing act of not always seeing things so black and white, but understanding that there are times when they are. Thus, the actions that any leader takes or doesn't take to answer the call of the black and white issues he or she may face can destroy their credibility, title, or worse yet their livelihood. The first to ask for forgiveness or the turning-of-the-cheek in most situations are those that we define as having a relationship. Leaders have to be able to separate the power of their position and their relationships to make the best decision in any situation. The responsibility is sometimes not an easy ordeal, because most charismatic leaders lead with heart and mind alongside their knowledge and skill. The best advice: never engage in the direct governance or supervision of a relationship that you feel so deeply about that it would make you question your best judgment. The last thing you want is for the situation to arise before you've learned how to separate these compelling and influential components in your life.

3.)Know that isolation should not be a state of good leadership.

My argument is not against relationships; it is for healthy relationships that do not stifle growth. You do not have to be a social butterfly to have great relationships with the people that you serve or who work within the same capacity as you. You have to be willing to engage in an authentic and meaningful way about the work that you do together. The sense of belonging that we all seek in life comes from the feeling that we are contributing to something and that something is also depositing back into our self. Leading in a bubble will only keep you capsulated in the intransigent beliefs that may be holding you back from an extraordinary you. You have to allow people to challenge you; to believe in you; to lead with you for your seed to flourish. Extrinsic motivation is just as mighty as intrinsic.

Relationships are paramount, but not if they veer you away from your pathway of achievement. Tread with caution on what relationships mean to you in your professional livelihood, and make sure that those whom you tilt your hat of approval to see the transparency in the link that you are establishing between the two of you.

Chapter 8: Make Greatness Your Sugarcane

Sugarcane has many purposes. I like to think of it as a multidimensional life resource. As a society, we personify greatness within what we achieve and what others produce. I think about the world of sports and how often the remembrance of a sports moment can bring us to tears. Those moments are classified as significant, one of a kind even, because they are.

Anything that moves you in a way that inspires you to see, do, or even believe that there is something beyond the life that you exist in that is fantastic- that is great- is remarkable. Everyone needs their sugarcane in life, but this is not a resource that is as easily accessible as purchasing it through a supplier. Your sugarcane is distinguished because it is self-grown and self-prescribed. It is significant to you and only you, and an abundant resource that impacts the advancement of your journey.

Finding your sugarcane:

1.)Pretending that you have something you don't, is not a prerequisite to leading.

As previously mentioned, discovering yourself is crucial to your pathway. If you are carrying proponents of yourself that require you to pretend to have and be all the things that you are not, you will miss the nurturing of the sugarcane that you naturally possess because YOU ARE SOMEBODY. There is so much more struggle to carry along your pathway when you have knowingly and purposefully established a persona of you that doesn't exist; this is the quickest way to dry up your resources because you never candidly had them. Good, bad, or ugly people will choose to believe in either version of who you are. Your wayward behaviors should not be the worse of you. We all carry baggage along our journey; this is the naturalist existence and noteworthy consideration that we have lived. The "made-up" baggage we take along is a boulder waiting to fall in your journey forward. Fertilize the sugarcane you already possess by presenting the best of you and nourishing the parts of you that you seek to grow. People can accept that you aspire for advancement, far more than they can concede that you have decided to become a stalemate in any state of being that affects their lives as much as your own.

2.)Be pretentious where you can and where it makes a difference.

We don't relish enough on seizing the moment; carpe diem your opportunities like they are scarce. If you haven't discovered where your talent lies or you have a fear of showcasing it- you are hindering the abundance of potential that your sugarcane can produce. I know nothing of the talents I don't possess because I never owned them. Hence, the purpose of being pretentious is not to take on something that you know little to nothing about; it's to embrace what you are knowledgeable about and what you can shine from within-outward to have a positive impact on something. I can't be an engineer; I don't have the skillset. I can't be a pilot; I don't know how to fly a plane. However, what I can be I know, and I know it well. Your pretentious self should not be something you fear; it should be something that you already are. Whether learned, developed, or a natural gene- you have the right to impress and deliver what you see as the superior part of you. Don't be closed mouth about the abilities that you already possess.

3.)Your sugarcane is fuel.

By this point, you should have assessed and owned your philosophy of leading and who you are. If you haven't this is an excellent place to stop and reassess, because what I am about to say is too simple for the mind that hasn't accepted that development is the consistency of self-growth. Energy is addictive. It is why we have a large market of products and beliefs that have created a multi-billion-dollar industry of what people see as "need" to produce or sustain their selves. The fuel that you have for what you do and why you do it provides the energy you have to embody to be manifest the remarkable you that you seek to be. For those that prefer the mediocrity of achieving anything, the energy will never exist. This combustion of zeal is different for everyone because we are all on our journey fueled by many similar and contrasting factors. What is essential is knowing that the maturation of your sugarcane will give you the fuel, the energy, you need to push forward in all that you desire to accomplish.

Greatness is an internal feeling that something that you've accomplished made a difference. It is the resource that provides, not just for self, but for others. It is giving's of our earning's.

Chapter 9: Culture is Relevant

P
erhaps, the most controversial topic of this book (sadly so) is to speak on the relevance of culture and advancement. What you either forget or decide not to take notice of will make you ill-prepared for the moment you have to be conscious and responsible for it; this is not a conviction of racial injustices or disparities. I am not an expert or experienced enough to speak on this topic to that degree. I have benefitted from the professional network of people of the same race and different races throughout my career.

However, what I firmly believe is that leaders should have a moral responsibility not to be divisive in giving equal opportunity to qualified individuals, no matter their cultural difference. All of us are a part of the experiences and people that contributed to our forward progress. For whatever the reason, if the experiences and the people you encountered along your journey didn't encompass diversity- situational and relational- then that is unfortunate.

Being different should not be a thwart in our progress. If nothing else, having people around you from different walks of life who can give credence to understanding the cultural significance of the livelihoods of others, is an asset. The argument, for me, is not that anyone should be given more privilege or clout because of the color of their skin- but no one qualified for consideration for an opportunity should be neglected because of it. The mentality you carry for embracing others who are different from you is one of the most influential components of character and integrity that you take through the various encounters with others in your life.

From my experience, I have found that people who are most uncomfortable with the relevance of culture were people who were afraid to be transparent about their ignorance of it. For instance, I know little to nothing about Japanese culture, other than the stereotypical assertions and minuscule historical facts that I have gathered through education. I am ignorant of the full scope of Japanese people culture. That ignorance is specific to Japanese culture, and a few other cultures and topics for that matter, because I am not all knowing about the things I haven't lived, observed, encountered, or studied vigorously. So, how do I recommend handling our ignorance in these situations?

1.)Recognize what's in your circle and what's not.

You do not have to pretend to affiliate with people that you are not, but you should be mindful about the people you surround yourself with and those that you do not. Perhaps, you don't have any people of different skin color or even a vastly different upbringing than you directly in your circle. Acknowledging this does not make you a wrongdoer, as we are all creatures of nature; our habitat is our comfort zone, and we naturally attract like-minded people into our circle and vice versa. It's the stifling of your intellectual growth that you must be mindful of disrupting. If we were to drop the subject of diversity from the context of race, culture,

43

religion, or status what would it be in the grand scheme of our thinking?

The state of being diverse is to have 'variety.' Education teaches us a variety of things. Circumstances and exposure can show us how to navigate a variety of situations. People teach us a variety of things. Thus, your circle, albeit similar or different, should encompass a range of knowledge and social awareness of the things you do and do not have some supreme expertise. Consult your circle to unveil what you may be missing in understanding people as a whole. The goal is to seek to understand what may be limiting your comfort with embracing the unknown, which could limit your ability to relate to all kinds of people under any circumstance.

2.)Separate the experiences that gave you biased perspectives.

We all have likely experienced an unfavorable situation with someone of another race, but similarly, we have probably had way more unfavorable experiences with those of the same race. Personify Newton's Laws of Motion to connect this philosophical thinking. If you are going somewhere or nowhere, you are at the mercy of interacting with an external force. In that collision, one energy over the other will feel a more significant impact from the encounter. However, the critical aspect of understanding about this law of motion is that unless you are compelled to change your state, you are constant; waiting for that external force to hit you. Forces of nature, whether those we collide with or that collide with us, can reenergize us and be teachable moments more than catastrophes.

We can learn from our rights and wrongs in every situation if we view the conflict or disagreement as to the real issue and not the components that can divide us as people. The things we carry forward in every situation shape the people that we are. We are bound to collide with our differences as much as our similarities; it is the law of life. Separating ourselves from the encounters that leave a bad taste in our mouth can pull our motion out of the constant state of viewing the impact of the unknown or undesirable from a stagnant state that does not improve our state of purpose. The breakthrough of this continuous state of epistemology (justifiable beliefs and opinions) that are distinguished from biases and solely reciprocated to gain a real perspective of the discord that impacts us is monumental. A jaded attitude can cause severance to your ability to make logical decisions. As a leader, defending your decision making is arguably more difficult than deciding on the action at times, and is at the core of what will produce success or failure. More than any other entity, decisions involving the treatment of people will be an essential component of the choices that you make.

3.)Be genuine.

Our interactions with one another are the most authentic moments that we can have to create connections that can lead to productive outcomes or the reversal of productivity. Attempting to be relatable at the moment that chaos or conflict transpires, is an erroneous presentation of character if it doesn't come from a sincere disposition. To the contrary, I know that these deceptive acts of leading and disingenuous moments exist. We decide who we are. We formulate our legacy with aura or temporary pomposity. Whomever you choose to be, know that our virtue is lived within not only how we treat others, but how we hold ourselves accountable to a standard of fairness even when we have to welcome the genuine ignorance that is sometimes required to own the earnest of fear when there is no rendezvous agreement.

Culture is relevant. Its relevance should have far less to do with the color of our skin, economic status, religious belief, or stereotypical norms created by society. Culture is relevant because it is the collective beauty of human intellectual achievements; not a plight of inheriting the most troublesome and sometimes horrific atrocities of the culture's in which we are born into, but to live within the betterment of our development and achievement because we exist in the homogeneous state of our culture.

Chapter 10: Fail Forward

T

he most challenging part of ending an opinion based personal memoir is that there is always so much more to say because the power in our words and self-reflection, is palpable. The point of anything written in this book is not to form your opinion, but to give you a perspective to draw your conclusions about your journey forward. I am an educator, you may or may not be; nevertheless, if you are seeking forward progress in any aspect of your life, I hope that you explore the thoughtfulness that is invaluable in reflecting and achieving your vision of success.

To wrap it all up (at least for now):

1.)Go for it.

Whatever it is that you want out of life, go for it. When you do, leave failure at the footsteps of your vision and make your picture of success the only thing that you are willing to accept in the falls that you will undoubtedly collide with as you strive for anything in life that requires dedication and effort. The force of a collision can suppress you or move you forward. How you embrace for impact, the good and the not so good, makes all the difference in how you toughen your armor for your journey ahead.

2.)Don't ask anyone to approve your vision.

It is easy for people to tell you that you can and can't do something that you believe in, because the voyage is yours-not theirs. So, at any time you seek advice you have a 50/50 chance of acquiring either end of those perspectives. It is not that advice and feedback shouldn't be sought or valued, but other people's opinion shouldn't become the opposition to your goals. Take the feedback you receive as information to access where you are, perhaps, and what you may have to hurdle to get to where you want to go. Receive, evaluate, and become methodical about the things that you carry forward from the advice in which you find useful. Whatever you do, don't isolate your vision by not allowing space for trustworthy advocacies. These can play a massive part in the extrinsic motivation that drives your success forward. Everybody needs a balanced cheerleader or two in life.

3.)Make the most at of the opportunities you have and anticipate those you have yet to see.

When you work, work hard and be good at it. When you are not working, work hard at being good at the life that you live. Life is compact in many ways: feel good, do good. There is no point in carrying detritus items or beliefs forward. These are often easier to site than even our very best qualities, which we sometimes shy away from; perhaps unconsciously, or out of fear that we may have to do something with the potential we possess. Be the best you that you can be — the best you; not someone else. The version of you doesn't need rebranding- it needs to be created, owned, and grown. The timing of opportunities is like the wind, always moving and present. When whatever is meant to happen for you is in your air be prepared by knowing you already rehearsed for it, and you are prepared to take ownership of what you've rightfully earned.

4.)Don't go it alone.

Your mind and heart are the most potent allies that you carry forward that don't cause you anything but acceptance and self-care. What success is that you will determine how you open your mind and heart. If success is something that is morally uplifting and astoundingly remarkable, your mind and spirit will be hand-in-hand on as you fall forward into the achievement meant for you. Feel for something the same way that you would expect it to feel for you. It would be selfish and utterly miserable to journey forward alone. Embrace the passion that exists within you.

5.)Lastly, be kind to yourself and others.

No explanation required.

About the Author

LaToya Easter is a native of Greenville, TX. She earned her bachelor's degree in Literary Studies at the University of Houston, and her Masters degree in Education Administration and Leadership at Grand Canyon University. She continued her education by completing her doctoral program at Grand Canyon University in 2016. This book will make the third publication for LaToya and the first in the non-fiction genre.

You can follow LaToya:@LaToyaEaster on Facebook, @Liv4ward on Twitter, @GirlDesperation on Instagram. You can also access her blog at www.liv4ward.net.

www.ingramcontent.com/pod-product-compliance
Lightning Source LLC
Chambersburg PA
CBHW071437040426
42445CB00012BA/1381